The Phoenix Living Poets

CONTROL TOWER

The Phoenix Living Poets

CONTROL TOWER

by

RICHARD KELL

CHATTO AND WINDUS

THE HOGARTH PRESS

1962

Published by
Chatto and Windus Ltd
with The Hogarth Press Ltd
42 William IV Street
London WC2

★

Clarke, Irwin and Co. Ltd
Toronto

© RICHARD KELL 1962
Printed in England at
The Westerham Press Limited

For my Mother and Father

Acknowledgements are due to the editors of the following, in which many of these poems have been included:

B.B.C. Third Programme
The Bell
Borestone Mt. Poetry Awards 1957
Fantasy Press Pamphlet 35
Icarus
The Irish Times
Irish Writing
Listen
The Listener
New Poems 1958 (P.E.N.)
New Poems 1961
The New Statesman
Outposts
Poetry Ireland
Rann
Threshold
Time and Tide
World Review

Contents

Chariots

Day was unkind to these,
Emphasising the sullen grime-etched face,
The droop of blinkered heads, the imperative bit,
Imposing a heavy load and a tortoise pace.

Dusk flicks a generous wand:
Like a reminiscence the empty coal carts spill
From the dimness as though from entombed antiquity,
To claim their lordly moment down the hill.

Four in a daredevil race
Pass dark shuttles of rhythm through twilight's loom.
These swaying taut silhouettes are bodies that sagged;
Indifference now has burst to a sudden bloom

Of zest. Sleek necks outstretched –
A rhyme of limbs where an ancient instinct moves,
Waking a ghost of thunder from dead arenas –
The horses spatter jewels from stabbing hooves.

Fishing Harbour Towards Evening

Slashed clouds leak gold. Along the slurping wharf
The snugged boats creak and seesaw. Round the masts

Abrasive squalls flake seagulls off the sky:
Choppy with wings the rapids of shrill sound.

Wrapt in spliced airs of fish and tar,
Light wincing on their knives, the clockwork men

Incise and scoop the oily pouches, flip
The soft guts overboard with blood-wet fingers.

Among three rhythms the slapping silver turns
To polished icy marble upon the deck.

Watchman

Over the injured ground
    Where pick and shovel probed –
Cutting away the soil
    Like flesh around the drain –
Over the jagged stones
    Red lanterns pin the dark,
And brazier-light forgets
    The solar glare of pain.

Loneliness, like the wind,
    Sneaks in: the watchman's mind
Grows draughty now. Across
    The brooding serious eyes
A twist of smoke uncurls:
    Gently the pipe-dreams rise,
The immaculate suave hotels,
    The music, the slim girls.

His thoughts lie low, fearing
    The infinite sky, the trees
Exposed like nerves to the wind's
    Abrasion, starlight spilling
Down the long approach
    Of love, to love's darkness,
That wears the lantern rubies
    Like a brooch.

Swans at Night

Into the brief reality
Of pallid lamps and grinning
Neon surveillance of the plunge
To pleasure, they are swimming,
Adagio of flutes
Over a heady counterpoint.
With the magic of a myth,
Quietly past the blunt
Knees of the bridge, rumpling
A redsilk circle of water,
They come from dream, coldly
Consummate into a smatter
Of warm half-living: as though
Forms of another reality
To which we are strangers here
In the plangent city.

Adolescence

A slinky fur of rain invites those lovers;
But hurts the young man wandering alone,
Whose fear and shame, bred of misinformation,
Curl like a tapeworm in the active will.

He has yawned away the routine hours,
Waiting for dusk to slide a copper sun
Into the night's juke-box, and travels now
The slick seductive pavements of his lust.

Friendly, concerned, the movie screen applies
An unguent music when the censor jabs.
Midnight he prowls his greenhorn wilderness,
Watching the lamplit whores he dare not touch.

Locked power disturbs him where the sour canal
Delineates his mood. (Those swans deceive
None who observed the yellow scum, the tins
Rusting among the weeds, the dead dogs floating).

A pit of darkness gouged beneath the sluice
Receives the trickling pus of dammed-up water,
Night after night recalling what befell
The swiftness and the clarity of love.

The Holiday Makers

Along the pier on lazy summer evenings
   They wander into leisure.
For this the day was made; they shall not feel –
   Haunting their easy pleasure
In talk of little things – the smouldering fear
   That broods like threat of thunder
Above the still horizon of tomorrow,
   For they have rested under
The gentle laws that sanction and renew
   Their talk of little things,
Like gulls their laughter light enough to move
   With slender glassy rings
Only the polished surfaces of selves.

   Cool in their eyes
The sea's flickering blue, the poised yachts.
   The curving sails surprise
A love whose gifted sight their lives have dazed.
   (Something here of scrolled
Petals that startle you from self-concern;
   Something of minds that hold
Desire away from the furnace of the heart
   Like wind precise and cold
Fashioned to these smooth contours). This way too
   They watch the mailboat swing
Beyond the pier, spading the water back,
   And lift their hands and fling
Goodbye, half gay, half sad, across the evening
   To friends they never met
But know exactly in the ritual moment.

This gesture will forget
How they betray the love that time recaptures,
    When neither carefree words
Nor petals nor a moulded wind can please them,
    And those white birds
Are folded in their grooves of rock. The selves
    They shaped with careful skill,
Artists of leisure on a summer evening,
    Elude the finest will.
The lonely yachts lie stripped like winter trees;
    Against the landing stage
The empty mailboat stands aloof and silent.
    And beauty turns to rage
Meeting those friends, who were eternal strangers.

Innocence

As children they would not compromise,
They spent their love and hate with swift conviction;
  Their glances told no lies.

For such pure egoists the name
Was quite irrelevant till some wistful tutor
  Carefully taught them shame.

And then it made some sense, for they
Discovered rival claims and clipped their passions
  And were no longer gay.

Where once with innocence they could turn
All things to their advantage, now they're thought
  Guilty of self-concern.

In small talk you will see their eyes
Flicker and fight, searching for love again
  And trying to tell lies.

Sidings

You'd hardly believe that half forgotten track
Had anything to do with crack express
Or labouring goods train. It does not end,
But pauses there: the colon buffers lend
An interim finality, as though
Fifty yards more or less were no
Matter for argument. Simply to be
Right there is pleasant – an inlet where the sea
Of industry and trade quietly laps
On grass and nettles, a flower or two; perhaps
A sparrow dances on the polished metals.

Sunlight and silence. Yet not unaware
When fists of smoke pummel the distant air
And the long locomotives thunder past,
Clattering over points: a seismic blast
Shudders across the network; the siding quivers.
But happy now with the music of a squat
Tank-engine shunting in the hot
And peaceful forenoon, clinking lines of trucks.

Those trains, those people. Travelling endlessly
The tedious circuits of economy.
It knows itself included (rightly so,
Owing its contribution). But they go
Too far, it thinks; they go too fast, and lose
Their souls in making money, making news.
Simply to be right here, alone, to make
A dream for wholeness' sake –
From sunlight, polished rails, a flower or two –
Is better in the long run.

Whistles blew;
The noise of luggage barrows, jets of steam
Slashing suddenly against the grain
Of reverie, clipped my thoughts into the plain
Square box of commonsense, which knows
That sidings presuppose
Something to be aside from. Do away
With that (so all can dream), and then you may
Destroy the gift of dreaming and create
A wilderness of tracks that merely wait –
With no through-lines to make them meaningful –
Watching the little engines push and pull
Backwards and forwards aimlessly all day,
Until the clinking music that they play
Sickens the ear with boredom. If you'd save
Those dreams, you must restore the plan that gave
The shunting relevance; and if you'd claim
Some value for your dreaming, scorn the tame
Refusal of the sidings, which invoke
The privilege of being where the stroke
Of pistons and the metre of the wheels
Are leisurely and mild, or distance feels
The impassioned emphasis of speed
A drowsy evocation, not a need.
Allow no anodyne for discontent,
But give the mind a structure taut and fine,
Guarding that clarity, that stillness where
All valid dreams begin.
                                    I paid my fare,
Boarded the train, secured a window seat
And sank into a wave of dust and heat;
Then, carried into sunshine, watched the trite

Unlovely town withdrawing out of sight,
Terrace by dismal terrace, lane by lane,
Mile after mile reciting the inane
Tautology of commerce.

                    I recalled
Those two soliloquies, and found the moral
Suspect either way. For there's no quarrel
Native here: no *ought*, but *is*, provides
The self that is not changed by changing sides.
Those were the facts – those hoardings, walls,
    backyards –
A nervous boredom my response. What guards
What clarity and stillness for what dream?
Merely an attitude, that may redeem
A sullen mood, but is as changeable
As moods themselves, answering to the pull
Of any clever argument it needs.
And what reflective programme that secedes
From high-powered competition saves a soul?
(To be right there is pleasant, not a dole
For moral indigence).

                  The beat of metal
On metal speeded up and the metre broke
Splintering over points. The punching smoke
Fattened and fluffed, then hovered down the line,
Thinning out to a drowsy evocation.
And never reached its proper destination,
The peaceful and idyllic, where a clink
Of trucks defined the stillness . . . Better think
Of something else. So much of me was there,
I must forget, or travel to despair.

Kierkegaard

'Without the risk, faith
is an impossibility.'

I have three plans to choose from on this island,
And every one a risk. Should I sail forth
With scant provisions in a tiny boat,
And set my course toward the crystal north,
Drowned or starved the loss I bear is double.
And so it is if I should seek the south,
Plodding through jungle, swamp and treacherous desert,
No wand of water touch my withered mouth,
And vultures pick the autumn from my bones.
If neither sea nor sand should make my grave,
But lazy I watch this palm tree dust the moon,
I tempt the fury of the tidal wave.

But no, he says; though three alternatives,
You have a single choice: to put to sea
And aim your bows toward the grim horizon,
While love is softly washing on the lee.
There is no time to rummage in reflection
Or lust and lounge with animal aplomb.
(The big green book lies open on my hand
And ticks away the seconds like a bomb.)

In the Beginning

God was the first poem ever uttered
By innocent astonished lips, when doubt
Had dropped a pebble in the water's trance,
The image of Narcissus cracked and rippled.
Then nothing was itself: always the hunters
Prowled through metaphor, felt it underfoot
Or brushing across their shoulders; saw it burst
Above the jungle, slash the trees with rain,
Dispensing love and anger like a giant.

And every poem was a souvenir
Of the unending trek toward perfection
(Lying surely beyond the steaming ridges,
The poisoned tracts of swamp). The eyes that once
Like emeralds caught the light of simple beauty
Were shaded now with terror, and the young
Smooth stems of thought crumpled and cut like
    thorn-trees.
And all day long among the voiceless flowers,
The sunlight's tilted pillars, parrots gossiped,
And screeched with laughter at the goggling idols.

The Burning Crate

Filled for the last time
The crate becomes a tank
Of liquid crackling gold,
And gives the thirsty mind
Refreshing light to drink.
Whose truth I would distil,
Yet all the words are cold:
Saying, earth's energies
Declare a holy will.

Suppose I walk away,
Wrench back when a sudden cry
Falls round me like a noose,
And see the taloned fire
Snatching a child at play:
Should this renew the spell
(All opposites reconciled)
Or instantly betray
A flaw, a casual hell
That mocks the power of choice
In man or simple child;
Invoke my hands, my voice,
Against the power that filled
The dark with life, and yet
As willingly destroys?

Though to love's urgency
I give my faith, being human,
The cold words haunt me still,
Teaching us to admire
Perfections that could kill

By accident in Eden;
And, from another myth
Correcting our despair,
To fuse the dying with
The pity and the fire.

A Supplicant Speaks of the Goddess Kwan Yin

She was a human thought, a dainty protest
Against the claims of godhead. We who loved life
And would have looked for truth in songs and flowers,
In wine and precious stones and women's beauty,
We could not take the Master at his word,
Close up the shutters while the sun was climbing
And light the lamp indoors. The wise men gave us paradox;
Some, being frightened by their cleverness,
Locked themselves in for ever and stuffed the windows;
And some allowed themselves a compromise:
Cherished the scents and colours in the garden,
Yet were penitent when they threw a glance
At the slim girls walking in the street.
But we, uncertain of the ways of God,
Too passionate or weak to crush desire,
Or else too much afraid of death (supposing
The wise men were deluded),
We took the risk of sin and prayed for mercy.

Here is the goddess, head graciously tilted,
Gentle and grave and wise, serenely smiling:
So we had come to think of her – a symbol
Of pure mercy. But sometimes I have seen
A little harlot demure and yet coquettish,
Her slender body made for men's hands,
And in the beauty of her brow and eyelids,
The pouting lips, the finger at her breast,
A hint of roguish humour and contempt.
It was as though we knew, in spite of all
Our glossy thoughts, the Master's way was best;

As though our souls betrayed us into truth,
Giving us back our dreams in this carved girl
With the sly face and small ambiguous hand.

Kwan Yin Gives Her Explanation

Sly and satirical you made me
As well as gentle and serene,
Harlot confused with blessed lady
Because the inner mind had seen
The truth you were evading.

Not that the Master's way is right,
But that you are fool and coward –
To have your sensual delight
And still avoid some moral hazard,
Praying when you take fright.

Kill the self-pity you named Kwan Yin,
Then call me lover instead of whore
And joyfully reinterpret sin.
Or smash my image, dance no more
And light the lamp within.

Firmament

Do not perturb the stillness of their faith,
Whirlpool of fire renew, spitting stars,
That long ago their sorrow clenched and pruned
Into a ball of gold. Manoeuvre this
Bright globe that you have made, though twice as
    powerful,
At tranquil distances from all the rest;
Or try a clash with one that's yet unrolled,
Still waving enthusiastic arms of light.

Had you come nearer truth it would be something:
But what have they revealed, these white explosions,
This blazing dialectic? You began
Adrift in space, and now, for all you've said,
You drift in space. And still that cold black sea
Awards no certain glimpse of land ahead.

The Quarrel and the Jester

Hardly as tall
Even as the kitchen table.
A pint-sized chucklehead
With a language of three words,
A blithe, believing eye,
A six-inch stride.

Something is going on
That's over his head. He trots
From knee to knee, drawing
Out of the unsuspected
Cold of the upper world
Familiar warmth.

And like the fool
(Without the fool's cunning)
Keeps out of politics:
When rival courtiers glare
Turns the indifferent glass
To any face,

Recalling there
The quaint humanity.
In his bright underworld
Something is going on:
He brings from fool to fool
Their common love.

A Word for My Son

I

Look, the first reel
Run off in memory, all
The bad bits cut away:
Discoveries, thrills – the feel
Of ice cream on your tongue,
The hop of a red ball.

Half hours of trains that sprout
From sleepy distances,
Bore through the wind, expand,
Smash your taut trance, a clout
Of steam-and-metal thunder
That crumbles, sifts, dies.

Barges down the canal,
Dock-leaves on glossy folds
Of water launched and lilted,
The sunned air magical;
By dandelion clocks
The timeless hours told.

You at the airport, spellbound.
Tension of noise and speed,
Slipstream playing the ground
Glissando: floated clear
On the smooth modulation
The sun-slicked wings recede.

Richmond, Windsor, Kew:
Long days of crowds and steamers,
Picnics and daffodils.
Your eyes alive with new
Puzzlements and convictions,
Your sleeping rich with dreams.

II

The deadlife now: the flint.
Rare things are filed away
Marked 'useless, treat with care',
The seemly trash we stint
And hate for reinstated.
A man has bills to pay.

A child has things to learn
Other than joy. (Not I,
Not any human being,
Authorised this). The turn
Of time leaves stinking pools
Where poisons multiply.

You four, I thirty-two:
I know but do not feel
The way you feel. That knowledge
Is my best gift to you
When love is mean, and pity
A construct of the will.

Yours is the same person
That prowled my ruined hours,
Fretting in shadows, dodging
The white floodbeam of reason.
By the same twist you change
And brood, contentment sours.

Watching you sulk and whine,
Your sense of wonder blurred,
Where shall I seek – knowing
The demon also mine
And you too young for knowledge –
The purifying word?

The Balance

Always the one that will not let me be –
When I would overflow (the mind free,
The heart ready to love, the voice to sing),
Reminds me with its prudent nagging tongue

That life is such and such: the free mind,
The loving heart and singing voice are kind;
So plan, cherish, be provident, pay the bills:

The horses lumber, but the tiger kills.

Always the one that will not let me change –
When I'd be careful, sympathise, arrange
(The voice level, the mind about to freeze),
Recalls what goodness tamed no longer sees,

That life is such and such: the frozen mind,
The level voice are to themselves unkind;
Then play, be prodigal, give joy its head:

The fountain's reckless, but the cistern's dead.

Encounter in a Reading Room

Good luck has entered, silky and black, padding
Slowly towards the desk where I sit reading.
And idly superstitious I think 'Supposing
She came to me, sensing that I'm uneasy,
Singled me out for comfort and change of fortune';
Yet know her poised contempt is all but certain.

Yes, like a brief sensation she goes by
And out of sight: why should she favour me
Among so many strangers with sorrows, fears
Like mine? I try to read – though feeling blurs
The glass of understanding time and again,
For all the will's concern to wipe it clean –

But look, she turns and springs, the logic gives
Beneath her sudden weight! And now she curves
And ripples in my arm, her grappling claws
Tear at my sleeve; the green uncanny eyes,
Slotted with black, distil an arctic glare,
And endlessly her soft vibrating purr

Winds intimacy off a reel of distance.
So she has come, indulging my pretence
Of singularity and special need.
And let her now pretend my gratitude
In one final amused caress, before
I drop self-pity gently on the floor.

Time for Clipping

On our arrival they were merely green
Needles pricking the soil, with space between
For air and sunlight; pride of the previous owner,
Who, dreaming a lawn quite innocent of weeds,
Had cleared the ground, sprinkled the fine seeds
And left the rest to fate and gardener's honour.

For thirty weeks they grew undisciplined,
Guzzling the rain and grappling with the wind;
Each juicy filament took the lean and swerve
Of its compacting wave in a churned lake.
At last, fetching the clippers and the rake,
I contemplate the sentence I must serve.

And then the blades move in, precise and swift,
Chopping the tough lank fibres, and a drift
Of shredded silk is loosed above the whish
And clack of the clean steel. In tangles wet
With hoarded rain – refusing to forget –
Their fragrance lingers like a mindless wish.

At length we make our survey: sodden dirt,
A stubble grimed, uneven, but alert;
And there the slugs and earthworms that remain
Through all retrenchments. Yet no real weed
Is trundled out of consciousness to feed
The slow impartial bonfire down the lane.

Poet on the Brink

Calm autumn night, seen from a high window.
Above the roofs, the trees, an urban sky
Breathed-on and fogged with light; a notched horizon
Printed black; spread behind leaves, transparent
Fans of lamp-gold; a clock-tower, white as bone,
Rapt in a floodlit trance; and over all
A gritty hush, a solvent monotone.

The clock strikes peace – and any moment now
West 3 will beg a sonnet. Just remember
What's going on down there, and let it beg.
Most certainly the very houses seem,
And all that mighty heart is lying – still.
Even amid such trees the fluting owl
Glides velvet through the darkness to his kill.

The Swan

Nothing more serene than the fluid neck,
The body curved like snow on foliage,
And spilt reflection moving smooth as oil.

But something wrecks the tranquil certainty:
The clean-cut shape unfolds; an evil wind
Tears its roots out of the fertile water.

The pattern's tugged awry – the neck rammed stiff,
Cumbrous wings whacking the startled air –
And terror swirls the surface of the lake.

The Woods

I

Semi-detached – how nice; with tiny gardens;
The paint so fresh and clean, the hedges trim.
Well-mannered avenues epitomise
The best of civilisation, don't you think?
Say, orderliness combined with charm and comfort.

   Perhaps. But notice especially the way
   The little roads end where the woods begin.
   A scarp of leaves towering above the rooftops
   Completes the emblem, points the paradox
   Of alienation and affinity.
   Nature endures, if only in the background.

How right you are. Men turn for sanctuary
To green retreats like this, as though to some
Residual innocence deep down in the mind.

   That wasn't –

May I see what it's like in there?
So peaceful and inviting. And so romantic!
Someone told me this was Dick Turpin country.

II

How dim and cool it is; and very quiet.

   People remove their talk, but not their litter.
   And why they have to use a woodland stream

To dump their scrap-iron in, I can't imagine.
Isn't the water *foul*. It's hardly moving.

But just look at those trees. I love the way
Their nets of foliage sieve the powdered sunlight.

For me there's something slightly ominous
In vegetable life so still and massive.
Do you remember how in fairy tales
The witches lived in woods?

Well yes – of course
I see what you mean. Yet, when all's said and done,
The trees are neutral: it is we ourselves –

At the weekends, and on bank holidays,
I'm told, this place is full of daring couples –

Where else could young love find, à la belle étoile,
Freedom so nicely blended with seclusion?

– And swarms with peeping toms. You mentioned
freedom:
Ten yards from here a girl was raped and strangled.
They found her sprawling in a pool of mud.

How horrible.

And this is where the schoolboys
Attacked the birds, destroyed their eggs, and stuck
Pins through the heads of fledglings.

No, please don't.
I think we'd better go.

All right – but don't
Go that way, if you're wise. There's something nasty
Around the corner, dangling from a twig.
It's been on view a fortnight. Some young lover
Left it, no doubt, to celebrate his manhood.

III

'Orderliness combined with charm and comfort'
I think you said? The woods, as we remarked,
Complete the fable. And when I see a man
Like that one, for example, with his paint-brush,
Or that one with his shears clipping the hedge,
I am reminded of the untrimmed thickets
His peeping thoughts frequent. And of the pins
Jabbing behind the laughter of his children.

Seeing Parkland from a City Train

There's no going back, even if we were sure
  Those origins are more than fanciful,
To green retreats where human life was pure.
But where was that clean break to justify
  Schemes that would make an alien of nature?
Though Yeats's golden bird disowns the sky,
The goldsmith is no clockwork curio;
  Being inventor, typifies the race
Whose fate was not to abandon, but outgrow.
As lively sons and daughters, growing beyond
  (And celebrating thus) their parents' skill,
Acknowledge all the same a family bond
By giving their affection and esteem,
  So it is good to prize what man constructs –
The hub of glass that swings the lighthouse beam,
The alert control tower and the viaduct –
  Rejecting only what was made to please
Some enterprising ape whose avarice mucked
Communities and landscapes by the score;
  Yet good, while praising these, to recognise
The long continuum that goes before,
Linking inventive mind, emotion, sense,
  To primal mystery. And we're right to dream,
When brain and limbs have earned their indolence
Working from what we know and can control,
  Into the mind's vaguer distances –
But sift the inklings from the rigmarole
Deadly with large oracular pretensions,
  For nothing is in focus at that range.
At least we learn by this our own dimensions;
The goldsmith cannot make a universe.

To set beside the leisured eloquence
Of water, branch and foliage, the terse
Comment of glass and steel, is natural.
    And seeing those city dwellers in the park
I envy them their ease, and wish them well.

The Pay is Good

A class of thirty student engineers,
Sixteen years old, disliked by all the staff.
Hearing about them at the interview,
And told to rule them with a rod of iron,
I tried my best but found I could not laugh.

He might be wrong. But I, no raw recruit,
Had found a proverb in a classroom war:
The peaceful sheriff proves that he can shoot
Before he throws his gunbelt on the floor.

A month or so of brooding self-distrust,
And then the moment came. I reached the door
(So this is it. Fight, for the love of Kell.
Show them who's boss – there's no going back –
    you must) –
And flung it open on the core of hell.

Somehow it worked. And they will never know
By what dissimulation it was done;
Or how the fuse of terror blasted out
Courage enough to master thirty-one.

Ode in Memory of Jean François Gravelet
Called Blondin

What do we think now of the Seven Natural Wonders!
Niagara has nothing to match your skill:
That huge splayed energy is inept as fat
Beside the strength whose terse and accurate jets
Could thread the eyes of needles. We have no comment
Equal to the occasion. More eloquent of amazement
The questions we should ask, though half suspecting
You would evade them, blind our understanding
With coloured flares of esoteric wisdom.

Are you exempt from fear, never to flinch
Knowing that a second from now your foot may skid,
Or a twitch of wind sway you the final fraction
Into the arc of death? Are you superconscious,
Quick as a turning diamond in the minute
Adjustments of your artistry – or entranced
And vested with infallibility
Like the somnambulist on the windowsill? –
Unaware of sunlight and cool air
And steamboats holding their breath; of multitudes
Legendary and silent attending miracles;
And drumming water, a precipice of foam
Crumbling away like dynamited chalk.

I think that you would laugh and say our minds
Were fluffy and whimsical; that your manoeuvres
Derive from no arcanum, but demonstrate
A rational and lucid gaiety.
So you extemporise on homely themes –

Trundle a wheelbarrow, bundle yourself in a sack,
Stalk on a pair of stilts; and to clinch the matter
You cook us an omelette and lower it onto a steamboat.

Ten thousand taut stares, and you poised at
    their vertex!
Puppet-master, gentle, omnipotent,
You hold us by those lightly tugging strings.
Like a dramatic chorus you present us
Exposed to one momentous circumstance,
Delineating man's complexity.
Let us admit the craving for sensation
And orgies of vicarious adventure;
The envy sizing up your power and pride;
Even the sense of horror that would suck
A curious pleasure from catastrophe.
And yet, a moment after you had fallen,
We'd wish to see you saved and reinstated.
Above all else we praise and cherish you
As steel-and-flint would praise the thunderstorm:
Your lightning is the splendid thrust that makes
A laughing-stock of death; we hit and run.

Showman you are, daredevil, virtuoso,
Greedy (who knows?) for money and applause.
These things we take for granted, but as part
And parcel of your genius.
The casual prodigies that you perform
Are not explained by motives so banal:
Mere egotism had safer ways to choose;
Only vocation could afford to take
Those skyhigh risks, and then to ask from danger
And skill's decisive act a pure delight.

Almost we see you fashioned for a strange
Provoking destiny: to celebrate,
By your most delicate and courageous art,
The clarity that blurs with routine boredom,
All grace and daring dreamed but unachieved.

I wish you the best of luck. May you tread your
        nimble highway
A thousand times and live your seventy years.
And may you die in your bed of a bad cold, confounding
The owl-wise oracles who have called you fool.

Citadels

That king spent fifty years or more
Holding the devil at bay;
Work was another name for war;
But then, growing grey,
He withdrew his men,
Thought the devil would scarcely
Trouble him again
Since they had fought so fiercely.
And in no time the enemy
Came swarming fresh from Hades,
Quietly took the city
And raped the golden ladies.

This one at the first surprise
Let the invaders in,
Allowed them to swank and fraternise
And soak themselves with gin;
And when they stank with pleasure,
Revealed at their most ghoulish,
Gravely took their measure
And found them rather foolish.
Disarmed them while they snored,
Prodded them back to Hades,
And feeling never so bored
Returned to his golden ladies.

Going Anywhere?

The limousine that Mr. L. S. Dee,
Tortured with ulcers and insomnia,
Works like a slave to earn enough to run,
Is indispensably related to
His job of marketing accessories
For the equipment used in setting up
The plant essential to producers of
An automatic measuring device
Particularly favoured by those firms
That specialise in intricate machines
For companies that make a certain type
Of electronic instrument designed
To regulate a mechanism required
By factories that supply materials
Used in the shaping of precision tools
Connected with the processes involved
In manufacturing refrigerators:
Cold comfort for such perishable foods
As now enrich the breakfast Mr. Grim
Savours without conviction, being sick
From an anxiety neurosis due
To his employment in the firm that made
The limousine that Mr. L. S. Dee,
Tortured with ulcers and insomnia,
Works like a slave to earn enough to run . . .

Fine Frenzy

The opening draft's injected by the muse –
Her medium, while entranced, being soft and porous.
She dries him then. He starts to pick and choose,
Bashing the daylights out of his thesaurus.

Perhaps. And yet, if muses are divine
And poets all too human, why the hell
Do opening drafts turn out so asinine,
While poems read superlatively well?

The medium is too earthy? That's fallacious,
For *Kubla Khan* came through without a hitch.
When trances are profound the muse is gracious,
But when they're shallow she's a perfect bitch.

No matter. Let the mind be dry or sopping,
It's still the finished product that's admired.
A line that cost the poet five days' chopping,
In fifty years will be his most Inspired.